Table of Contents

The Unseen Science of Overcoming Stress

Moment-By-Moment

By Andrew Bloch

The TRUe breaTH™ Disclaimer:

The intention of the TRUe breaTH™ ebook is to share a new paradigm and to help people deal with stress. As with anything new, however, it is always compared to the current model. It is not our intention to bash any medical health practitioner.

I encourage everyone to find or continue to learn from mental health professionals, life coaches, mindfulness practitioners, yogis, and/or meditators. These healers use fantastic time-tested methods to continue to look inside. I *love* these professionals and I *love* these methods, and they are absolutely necessary and vital to your overall health and well-being.

Introduction: Welcome to TRUe breaTH™

For some people, just hearing about breath work can seem scary or overwhelming. I can reassure you that this doesn't need to be the case, particularly with TRUe breaTH™. Whether you are an avid daily practitioner of meditation or you never have meditated a day in your life, this course is for you. The process of understanding and applying TRUe breaTH™ is simple and you will be able to use it immediately after reading this ebook.

Even if you don't necessarily understand the reasons or how it works, you will see a profound *difference* in *your* life. And the best part is that you don't need any equipment or special training. TRUe breaTH™ can be taught and used by anyone, from young children to our mature population. Life is stressful and filled with so many pressures—learning TRUe breaTH™ is not meant to be one of those stressors. It's meant to be easily performed in your daily life to *transform* you, *MOMENT-BY-MOMENT.*

My name is Andrew Bloch, and I've been practicing in the medical field for over 30 years as a physical therapist, athletic trainer and acupuncturist. My expertise is holistic solutions for chronic pain. In addition to TRUe breaTH™, I developed my own systems called Reflexive Pattern Therapy™ and Color Mapping™ to help people to feel better immediately.

A major component of my system to treat chronic pain is knowing that stress plays a huge role in causing your body to be in pain in the first place. In fact, pain is similar to stress and stress is similar to pain. I learned a lot about stress by treating chronic pain. I want to divide stress and pain into two different categories, the *seen/structural* and *unseen/non-structural.*

TRUe breaTH™ is a combination of western structural *seen* knowledge, and eastern *unseen* energetic wisdom. I know that's a mouthful, and I'll explain it in a way that makes it easy to understand.

To help you understand this concept, here are some examples of the relationship between these two categories and pain and stress.

If a person in pain asked, "What is causing my pain?" the answer depends on who they're asking. A physical health practitioner who was asked this question would think something is wrong with the *structure*, since to them, the pain is *seen*. A physical health practitioner could be a physical therapist, massage therapist, chiropractor, trainer—anyone that uses the body or *structure* (the *seen*) to treat people in pain.

If the same question, "What is causing my pain?" were asked to a mental health practitioner, they would say that something is wrong with your head or your thoughts, since to them, the pain is *unseen*. A mental health practitioner could be a counselor, social worker, psychologist, psychiatrist, life coach—anyone who works with emotions or *non-structure* (the *unseen*) to treat people.

The patient's pain can be *seen/structural* to the physical health practitioner, or *unseen/non-structural to* the mental health practitioner. With pain, those are the two categories.

Now let's look at the similarities between stress and pain. If a person is stressed and asks a physical health practitioner, "What is causing my stress?" the practitioner would say something is wrong with your structure. Maybe you were lifting too much weight, so there is an issue with the structure or the "seen stress."

If the same question was asked to a mental health practitioner, they would say that something is wrong with your non-structure. Maybe the issue is your way of thinking, so there is a non-structure or *unseen* stress.

An important aspect of understanding TRUe breaTH™ is that unlike a physical or mental health practitioner who only sees one side or the other, we will look at *both* categories; the *seen/structural* and the *unseen/non-structural* together, to improve your ability to *deal* with life *moment-by-moment*.

Reflexive Pattern Therapy, which is my system for treating chronic pain, stimulates the nervous system to reset the brain and instantaneously boost a patient's ability to deal with pain. TRUe breaTH™ works in the same fashion to stimulate the nervous system and reset the brain, which will instantaneously improve a patient's ability to deal with stress.

At present, the most popular methods for dealing with stress are mindfulness and meditation. While these are great systems, in my opinion they unfortunately exclude too many people. These methods can take hours of people's time, can be difficult to grasp the concepts and techniques, and you might not even notice any difference. Often when I ask a patient if they meditate or do mindfulness, they respond that they would like to, but they don't have the *time* or want to put in the *effort* it takes to learn.

I want to reiterate that my intention here is *not* to bash mindfulness or meditation. In my experience, there are far too many people that mindfulness and meditation do not work for. I would encourage you, if mindfulness and meditation *do* work for you, continue to use these techniques. I'd actually recommend you to perform TRUebreaTH™ to enhance your practice of mindfulness or meditation, since they work well together.

Even though methods to treat stress might be controversial. I think everyone can agree stress is a major influence that's affecting our health and wellbeing. Stress is not going away any time soon and for most of us it's increasing *daily*.

Stress is defined as a feeling of emotional or physical tension. Stress equals tension and tension then can be either emotional (which is unseen/non-structural) or physical (which is seen/structural), or both emotional and physical.

Stressors are defined as reasons we experience a feeling, which can be due to family, job, or relationships.

Combining the two, **stress** is a feeling of emotional or physical tension ***caused*** by a **stressor**.

TRue breaTH™ is not about decreasing your stressors, which can be very difficult or impossible to change. Stressors are things like relationships, family, location, occupations, and so on that are not easily changed; these are some of the biggest stressors (or what I call the *whys*) in people's lives.

TRUebreaTH™ focuses on helping the body *deal* with stress or tension generated by the emotional unseen/non-structural component of life.

So, let's get started to teach, to learn and to demonstrate TRUe breaTH™.

Chapter 1: Who Are You? The Foundation of TRUe breaTH™

Exercise 1: Notice

The most important part of TRUe breaTH™ is to *notice*. Take the next 30 seconds to just *notice* how you breathe.

Cadence: I AM... 5 seconds

GRATEFUL... 5 seconds

COURAGEOUS... 5 seconds

HAPPY... 5 seconds

KIND... 5 seconds...

Part 1: Notice Your State of "Being"

Even though it was only 30 seconds, this is the initial process of practicing your ability to *notice*.

- First, *notice* that you're actually breathing; *that's great news*.
- Second, *notice* how you're breathing:
    - Do you *notice* if you're using the neck, chest, or belly?
    - Do you *notice* having to do anything to breathe?
- Third, did you *notice* any thoughts or feelings *before* or *during* your breathing?

Realize that noticing is an active process. For this chapter, our focus is the third point: To *notice your feelings* and witness what's happening on the inside. In the 30-second exercise that we just completed, notice the words in the sequence.

Cadence:

I AM...

I AM... GRATEFUL...

I AM... COURAGEOUS...

I AM... HAPPY...

I AM... KIND...

These words are all states of "being." Now you might be saying, "What the heck is a state of being?" I was introduced to the concept of "being" over 20 years ago and it took me about 10 years just to understand what they were even *talking about,* and even longer to figure out *how* to utilize it in my life. Being has to be *experienced.* For example, think of a rollercoaster. I can talk, show and write about it...but the ride needs to be *experienced,* and that experience is *so* hard to describe.

Part 2: Wishes and Wants Don't Work

The current process of life is what I call *Having > Doing > Being*. Most of us process life starting with a thought, *wishing or wanting* to have something, whether it be money, success, relationship, family, or a specific occupation.

Then we start *doing* things in hopes that we get our *"haves," our wishes,* and *our wants.* Let's use the example of *wishing or wanting to "have" money*—certainly that would be a great "*have*" for most of us. We "*want" or "wish" for money,* we then start to *do* things in hopes to *"have"* more money, like getting a formal education, working more, investing, getting mentored, reading books, doing whatever it takes to *"have"* money.

Your state of "being" is then determined by whether you "*have*" money or you don't "*have*" money.

Now if you didn't "*have*" the money you wanted or wished for, then your state of "being" could be anything from sad to angry. And even if you *did* have money, that money doesn't necessarily get you the state of "being" that you desire because money doesn't necessarily bring you happiness. So there are plenty of people that *have* money and are, unfortunately, still sad, depressed, angry or anxious.

This is a typical example of the *Having > Doing > Being* process of life.

If money is not your "*wish*" or your "*want,"* then you can replace "*money*" with an occupation, relationship, or whatever it is that you "*wish*" or "*want*" to have.

Mindfulness, visualization and law of attraction are some of the methods based on this *Having > Doing > Being* process of life. In my humble opinion, these methods haven't worked for the masses, since so many people are still suffering or trying to figure out how to find their "purpose" in life.

Let's try an example for yourself. Choose one thing that you wish or want. Your "*have.*"

___

Then write down some of things that you would hypothetically *do* to get your "*have.*"

___

Then write down your anticipated state of "being."

___

I hope it was hard to come up with your state of "being" to solidify the point that your state of "being" was determined by whether you did or didn't obtain your "*have*."

Part 3: BEING < Doing << HAVING

We need to do the opposite. BEING **<** Doing << HAVING

Being means just *noticing* your feelings. *Noticing* if it's a positive feeling like happiness, or *noticing* if it's a negative feeling like fear.

This is a state of "being." Keep in mind that this is totally your own opinion, so you're never wrong. If you *"notice"* fear, for example, *stop* and just *"notice"* your feeling.

Most importantly, you don't need to do anything except *"notice."* This is ancient wisdom for the modern person to utilize while living your life. The initial step is for you to start to develop your skill of *"noticing," moment-by-moment.*

Let's look at how we can use TRUe breaTH™ and the principles of BEING **<** Doing << HAVING. Once you *"notice"* that your state of being is negative—meaning you want to feel something else—you should immediately focus on your breath. Without doing anything or judging your negative feelings, just breathe any way you want. Then you can start to *do* things like work, study, talk, exercise, etc. And eventually, you will have everything and anything—including your purpose in life.

Read and do the exercise in this chapter over and over, because each time you will have the possibility for a greater understanding of BEING **<** Doing << HAVING and a new perspective on life.

Chapter 2: Automatic...Systematic

<u>Exercise 2: The State of "Being" Breathing</u>

This exercise is to gain control of your "*noticing*" and your "physicalness."

You're going to sit still for one minute. If you can't do that, sit still for 30 seconds.

Before you start, take a moment to *notice* and write down your positive or negative state of "being."

Remember, you're never wrong and there is no judgement or "doing."

1. Sit with your hands and feet in a comfortable position. Ideally, I'd like you to sit up straight, with your back off the chair so you aren't reclining, and just sit still.

2. Sit completely still for one minute, meaning no movement at all. In sitting completely still, you might start to "notice" that you want to itch your face, rub your eyes, need to sneeze, or that your hands are too hot or too cold.

   My point is, when you sit still and you start to "notice." Not only do you "notice" all of these physical things that you didn't realize before, but also that your mind will start to "race" with all the things you "need" to do.

a. You'll also "notice" all of the negative judgmental feelings about just "noticing," such as "this is a waste of time" or "I have so many things to do."

b. And the craziest thing is that this is all in one minute.

c. Could you imagine if you had to sit like that for 15 or 20 minutes?

Part 1: Introduction

Now that you are "*noticing*" your breathing, know that "*noticing*" takes action. It takes presence to *notice* who you are and your state of being, *moment-by-moment,* which depends on your stressors of life and your environment.

Let's discuss the complex central nervous system and *which* system we should use to create *transformation*.

Now, using the words "nervous system" and "complex" can cause stressors for some people, so just take a moment to *notice:* Did they cause a difference in your state of being? Did you go from *excited* to being *anxious*? Just "*notice.*"

Using typical medical terminology, your state of "being" can *shift*, even though you're not aware of it. It's my intention to take complex deep "knowledge" and "wisdom" and make it *easy on the ears*.

In most other professions, this isn't a new concept—in the tech world, for example, they *simplify* the simplest things; even something like *hailing a cab.* In the medical profession, however, it seems like the opposite.

When practitioners use medical terminology that patients don't comprehend, (in my opinion) I think that those patients are *consciously* admiring that practitioner, but *subconsciously* the patients are scared, anxious, and shaming themselves for not knowing what he or she means.

In the next few chapters. I will be simplifying some complex scientific and philosophical concepts.

I am simplifying these concepts on purpose and *consciously,* you might *not* be admiring me since I might not sound intellectual (which I'm okay with), because hopefully *subconsciously*, everyone reading in this TRUebreaTH™ ebook will feel safe and secure in its terminology that's easily understood.

Part 2: The Automatic Nervous System

Our central nervous system is divided into two systems. One is called the voluntary nervous system and the other is the involuntary nervous system.

One nervous system, the voluntary nervous system, works when you want it to "work," as you can see from its name. It mostly functions to move the musculoskeletal system. After all, our hands and feet don't move on their own. The musculoskeletal voluntary nervous system allows us to *consciously* take care of ourselves from the time we wake up until the time we go to bed; we think about it and then do it.

This is very different from the involuntary nervous system, which works automatically without "*thinking*" about it. This involuntary nervous system, or what I have renamed the automatic nervous system, is mostly made up of the organs, such as the heart, liver, spleen, kidney, and lungs. Its function is to manage digestion, heartbeat, breathing etc...

Just take a second to just contemplate how incredible the automatic nervous system is. Seriously, there isn't a word in any language to describe the *awesomeness* of the automatic nervous system. It instantaneously works 24/7/365 without you ever thinking about it. So I'm going to ask you a question...

If you were going to choose between the nice functional voluntary musculoskeletal nervous system or the *awesome incredible* automatic organ nervous system, which one would you think would we use to create *transformation*? I know it's a leading question, but I want the automatic nervous system to stand out as *the* system for *transformation*.

Part 3: The Transformational Organ

The automatic nervous system predominantly manages the organs of the body. Let's think of some of the organs—heart, liver, spleen, kidney, and lung—and realize that they all work on their own without any *conscious* thought.

After eating something, whether you think about digestion or not the digestive organs are going to digest the food. In fact, all the organs work in the same mechanism. There is, however, one organ in this magical automatic nervous system that we can consciously control if we want to, and without years of training. So, I have another (not so leading) question... If you had to pick an organ that you could have some control of in the automatic nervous system, which organ would you choose?

The answer is the lungs and the action is breathing—hopefully the title of this ebook gave you a hint.

The automatic organ system is the nervous system for *transformation,* and the *transformational* organ is the lungs.

Chapter 3: It's All About Connection

So far, we have discussed the automatic nervous system, the organs and the lungs. This is mostly about the western structural *seen* knowledge. Now we are going to start the exciting part, combining what we already have learned with the eastern *unseen* energetic wisdom.

Part 1: Difference between Emotions and Feelings

I'm sure you have heard the terms feelings and emotions, but do you know the *difference*? A fundamental difference between **feelings** and **emotions** is that **feelings** are experienced *consciously*, while **emotions** manifest *either consciously* or *subconsciously*.

According to the TRUe breaTH™ system, feelings are experienced in the voluntary musculoskeletal system and emotions are experienced in the automatic organ system.

Everyone's life experiences and traumas are completely different and thus feelings are different, since everyone interprets their life experiences differently.

Part 2: Location of Emotions

In western medicine, the seven emotions are: anger, fear, disgust, happiness, sadness, surprise, and contempt, and they are believed to be housed in the brain. Part of TRUe breaTH™ is applying eastern energetic unseen wisdom, which states that emotions are not housed in the brain but in the *organs*. The ancient healers might not have called it the "autonomic nervous system," but they definitely knew the importance of the organs and their relationship to *emotions*.

The five emotions paired with the organs are:

1. Liver = Anger
2. Spleen = Judgement
3. Heart = Joy
4. Lung = Sadness
5. Kidneys = Fear

This might not be an easy concept to accept, but remember we need a new paradigm to create *transformation*.

The ancient healers knew that the organ automatic system consisted of the seen/structural aspects, as in the actual organs (like the lung). But, more importantly for us, they understood that the organ automatic system also had an unseen/non-structural aspect in the *emotion* of the organ (for the lung example, the corresponding emotion is sadness).

This is a very important concept to accept: that there is an unseen/non-structural aspect and that we need to tap into this magical wisdom. If breathing is the portal to your emotions, then emotions can be impacted by the way you breathe.

Whatever your life experiences and traumas are, everyone can *utilize* their automatic nervous system, via the lungs, to access their *unseen emotions*.

Part 3: Energetic Emotional Connections

Now that you are aware of the unseen/non-structural connection between the organs and emotions, the ancient healers also taught us about other profound connections between the *seen/structural* and the *unseen/non-structural.*

From the point of conception until death. *We as humans are meant to connect.* We ourselves have numerous seen/structural connections and, as you're starting to learn, we also have many unseen/non-structural connections.

In my western medical background, I understand the seen/structural aspect of connections quite well. The ankle bone is connected to the knee bone; the knee bone is connected to the hip bone...and you know the rest of the song.

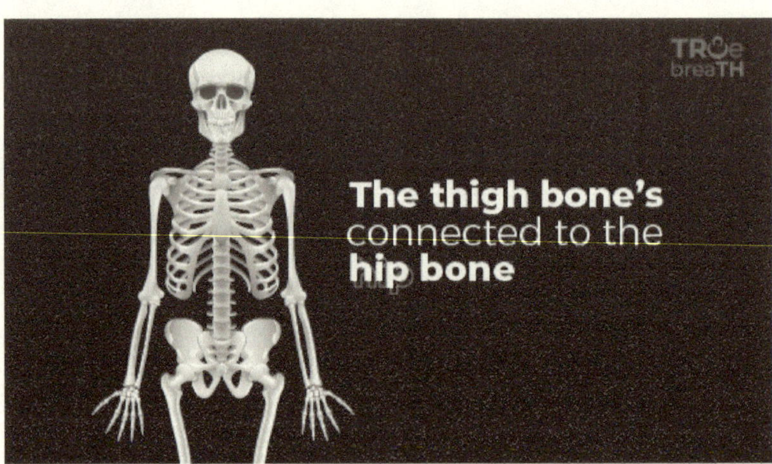

Part 4: The Embryological Model

The embryological model is a combination of eastern wisdom and western knowledge—just like TRUe breaTH™.

It starts with an understanding of western embryology; that a sperm and egg connect and form one cell. From that process it goes through what's called cell division, where one cell splits to become two identical cells; then four identical cells and then eight and so on, always doubling. They are all identical cells that split off, yet we are not all identical cells.

From there, our cells begin to separate or disconnect, which is called ***cell differentiation***.

Our cells are no longer identical, but we have similar seen/structural connections and relational unseen/non-structural connections...until we eventually become a baby.

In this process of cell differentiation, our hands eventually separate or disconnect from our feet; our wrists from our ankles; elbows from our knees; and hips from our shoulders.

This is why they look very similar.

It's interesting and easy to visualize the seen/structure connection in our hands and feet since they look so similar—*five fingers, five toes.*

But what is fascinating and harder to visualize is the eastern unseen energetic connection. The hands and feet are not only physically connected, they are also energetically connected. The hands and feet work together, energetically.

Chapter 4: The Belly: Connection and the Embryological Model

What do you think is the greatest *unseen/non-structural energetic connection to the organs*?

It's the belly to the brain.

Exercise 3: Belly Breathing

This exercise is all about learning to breathe with your belly. Nobody likes to stick out their gut, so it will feel *uncomfortable and unnatural,* but it's *very* necessary.

Let's go through the step-by-step process of belly breathing together. First listen and watch the exercise and then we'll do the exercise together.

Start by lying down, since this is the easiest position to learn belly breathing.

1. *Notice* your state of "being"
2. Close your mouth
3. Eyes open
4. Put your tongue on the roof of your mouth
5. Place your hands on your belly
6. Breathe in through your nose

7. As you breathe in through your nose, stick your belly out

8. Breathe in as much as you can

9. Push your belly in to your hands as big as you can (think of Santa Claus)

10. Do your best not to use your chest or neck muscles—only your belly moves

11. Hold your belly breath

12. Then, exhale your breath out of your mouth

How did it go? I know this can be an unnatural way to breathe, but keep at it since breathing is one of the key components for *transformation*. Once you get the hang of this, try to do the belly breathing exercise in different positions such as standing and then sitting.

The goal is to be able to belly breathe in any position during the day.

Part 1: Your Gut Feeling: The Unseen Connection of the Belly-Brain

As we talked about in Chapter 3, the embryological model isn't just a structural model of the hands and feet looking similar. There is also a relational component, an unseen/non-structural energetic connection. The same can be said with the organs and the brain. If you squashed all the organs together to the size of a cantaloupe—the size of your cranium—the organs would now, look like a brain.

You've probably heard the question, "What is your gut feeling?" In Chinese medicine, your gut or your intestines are seen as your second brain.

Comically, modern science is finally catching up with ancient wisdom to now tell us that there are more neurons in the intestines than the brain.

This continues to validate the eastern energetic unseen wisdom that emotions reside in the organs and not the brain, as commonly taught.

Part 2: Location of the Mind

Modern western medicine has never been able to identify where exactly the mind is located. I find this point very interesting since so many medical and mental health practitioners talk about the power and detriment of the mind. My belief is the location of the mind is not as important as the *acceptance* that the mind functions within the voluntary musculoskeletal mind-brain system

The mind/brain works from past events and traumas and reacts from the past. When stressors come into your life, the mind/brain considers past events or traumas to determine if those stressors are stressful, and uses the past to dictate what you are going to do in the present moment and in the future.

The reason this is so important is that if we keep using the voluntary musculoskeletal mind-brain, we are just repeating our past *over and ove*r in an attempt to create *transformation* in the present moment, and this system leads to more suffering.

The voluntary musculoskeletal mind-brain is built for protection based on your past positive or negative experiences. It's absolutely invaluable if you decide to do something dangerous like crossing a busy street (for the obvious reasons); it is not, however, built for *moment-by-moment transformation*.

The problem is that the stressors of current life that we protect against are not just as simple as crossing a busy street *any more*. Stressors of life are enormous, and start when you wake up. Your kids, your job, your relationships, your phone, your daily life, your purpose. It never ends from the time you wake up until you go to bed—and some even as you sleep.

In a mindfulness approach, you are noticing your thoughts and trying to quiet your mind, which is not easy to outright impossible.

We use TRUe breaTH™ to access the automatic organ *soul*-brain system to create *transformation*.

After "*noticin*g" your state of "being," now notice which area of your body you are using to breathe.

Part 3: Laugh Your Way to Transformation

Western medicine has another name for the gut called the solar plexus; maybe the ancient healers called the gut the "SO*U*L"ar plexus with a *"U."* Solar or SOULar plexus refers to the light or looking inside to find enlightenment in your organs, which I call *soulfulness*.

Enlightenment, or finding the light within, is the basis for the teachings of Budha, who was one of the originators of meditation and mindfulness. The Buddha is a symbol within meditation, and there are different representations in painting, statues and figures.

One representation of the Buddha is of the Indian monk.

Looking at the image through the eyes of mindfulness you notice that he's slender, tight-lipped, his eyes are closed, his head is more prominent and, to me, he looks uncomfortable.

The story goes that Buddha spent years in solitude, "noticing" and looking within himself to ultimately attain enlightenment, to find his light, his truth, his purpose.

Unfortunately, in our busy everyday lives, most people don't have the ability to spend large portions of each day meditating in hopes of finding enlightenment.

Looking at the image through the eyes of TRUebreaTH™ and soulfulness, we use a different representation of Buddha. The image is of Budai, who was a Chinese monk in the 10th century. He is referred to as the laughing or weight-challenged "Buddha," just to be politically correct.

You can notice that he's out of shape, laughing, eyes open or squinting, big belly and, to me, he looks comfortable and happy. I believe the two images are a visual metaphor that represents the unseen/non-structural energetic belly-brain connection.

Looking at the size of the laughing Budai's belly compared to the head of the Buddha, you notice that the Budai's belly is twice as big as the head of the Buddha. I'm convinced this is a map for *transformation* or *enlightenment*.

The terms spirituality or *enlightenment* can be controversial, but for me, it is the human spirit that is all about free will and the soul which resides in the organs. We need to think of how we can improve and strengthen this human *spirit* to help defeat the mind.

I have heard terms such as the "power of the mind" or "mind over matter," which I believe are misrepresented since the mind, in modern stressful times, is useless for the masse, to attain *transformation*. Utilize the belly—where the soul is located—rather than the head where thinking takes place.

This shows that the belly is *twice* as important as the head. The Budai's belly represents TRUe breaTH™ *soulfulness*, and the Buddha's head represents *mindfulness.*

That is my own metaphoric interpretation of the spiritual aspect of connection, and how we can use this eastern wisdom to create *transformation* or enlightenment *moment-by-moment*. You don't need to wait minutes, weeks, months or years sitting in solitude.

Part 4: Importance of the Belly

We've established how important the belly is during breathing, yet it is something that you don't really notice in everyday life unless you focus on it.

If you see or speak to someone when they're stressed, such as at work, in a stressful meeting or as I do with patients, often they will "sigh" or breathe as though they are catching their breath from running a marathon, even though they haven't moved anywhere.

This is because they've run a marathon of *unseen* stress, such as judgment, worry, or fear from the stressors of life.

What is interesting here is that there are only two muscles that are innervated off the brainstem below the neck; every other muscle in your body below the neck is innervated off the spinal cord. The two muscles are the trapezius in your upper back and your sternocleidomastoid, which is on the side of your neck.

The reason I tell you about the trapezius and sternocleidomastoid is they not only work *voluntarily*, like every other muscle, but they also have the ability to work automatically because they are involved with breathing. These two muscles work based on the stressors of life, whether those stressors are seen or unseen.

The unseen stress of life, such as judgement, worry, or fear, can cause you to use the chest and neck for breathing or sighing. Unchecked, this pattern could be keeping you in these negative states of being. This is the reason not to use the neck and chest muscles at all during TRUe breaTH™.

Remember, before you breathe, take inventory inside yourself to notice, on a *moment-by-moment* basis. Use the metaphor of the Budai, and breathe through the belly to connect with your emotions and your soul. Make sure not to use your neck or shoulders. Now we just need to add the *magic*...

Chapter 5: Why Reflexes? It's Just Magic

Exercise 4: Expanded Belly Breathing

It's very important to breathe through the belly, so let's see if you can *deepen your awareness* of the belly during breathing.

Here are the steps:

Last time we started by lying down (since it's the easiest to learn). This time if you want to challenge yourself, you can use different positions like standing or sitting. *Let's do it.*

1. *Notice* your state of "being"
2. Close your mouth
3. Eyes open
4. Put your tongue on the roof of your mouth
5. Place your hands on your belly
6. Breathe in through your nose
7. As you breathe in through your nose, stick your belly out
8. Breathe in as much as you can
9. Push your belly in to your hands as big as you can (think of Santa Claus)
10. Do your best not to use your chest or neck muscles—only your belly moves

11. Hold your belly breath

12. Then, exhale your breath out of your mouth

Great job; hopefully it's becoming more natural.

Part 1: Organs Are Built for Speed

The magic only works if you stick that gut out.

I've always been *fascinated* with magic. The concept that I'm seeing something I know is real, and then that something is instantaneously unseen amazes me every time. This mixing of the *seen* and *unseen* gives you an idea of my own passion behind TRUe breaTH™.

For magic to work it's transformational, not change. The difference between *transformation* and change is time. *Transformation* is instantaneous and change takes time—hours, days, weeks, months, years and, unfortunately, infinity for some of us.

You don't *transform* from being overweight to thin, you *change*. We all know this doesn't happen instantly, so the whole idea is that *speed* is really important. Time often limits people from practicing meditation, as it is traditionally a slow process and people want solutions fast.

We are all born with an automatic organ nervous system that is built for *speed* and instantaneous results.

There is nothing *magical* about change.

Part 2: Reflexes and Magic

With TRUe breaTH™ the magic is using our own innate reflexes, which travel at the speed of light and bypass the mind-brain. You might have heard the term "Godspeed," that refers to healing at a miraculous rate of time.

We can utilize "'Godspeed" by stimulating our own body's innate reflexes, using our ability to respond to this stimulus without a second thought. It happens *instantaneously* and is NOT based on your past experiences or trauma's. Using reflexes is *moment-by-moment*.

The belly-brain reflex is my own personal terminology and I define the **Belly-Brain Reflex. (physiology) as: An innate unseen non-structural energetic connection (discussed in Chapters 2 and 3) between the belly and brain and, when stimulated via deep belly breathing according to the principles and techniques from TRUebreaTH™ (discussed in Chapter 4), will cause a reflex resulting in an immediate automatic downregulation to the central nervous system.**

The magic just happens—science sometimes takes time to catch up with wisdom.

If you need to consciously think about something using your brain, your thoughts, your mind, it's a slow process for change to occur. The *magic* of using our Belly-Brain Reflex is to do it without conscious thought—it is at Godspeed, the speed of light and is *transformational, moment-by-moment.*

Part 3: Feel Better Get Well: The New Paradigm

Before we put everything together that we have learned and experienced so far, I want to present a paradigm shift in meditation, medicine, business and life. TRUe breaTH™ was created with a new paradigm called *Feel Better* Get Well. On the contrary, meditation and mindfulness use the opposite paradigm of "Get Well *Feel Better*."

This current paradigm isn't wrong; in fact, it has helped many people. But it's also not right for the masses.

The current paradigm focuses on noticing your stressors and the feelings that are generated. Then once you know the "why," you need to meditate/practice mindfulness for hours, weeks, months in hopes of eventually *feeling better*. From what we have already discussed, this is a paradigm based on change.

The new paradigm of *Feel Better* Get Well focuses on using the *magic* of reflexes, the autonomic nervous system, and belly breathing to bypass the mind/brain/thought complex to instantaneously transform your state of being so you *feel better* immediately. Then and only then can you look at your stressors or your "whys" and eventually Get Well.

The great news is that mediation and mindfulness *absolutely* have a place in the new paradigm, it just comes after you *feel better* by performing TRUe breaTH™.

Chapter 6: What You Learned About TRUe breaTH™

Exercise 5: TRUe breaTH™

Utilizing all of the principles in the past five chapters, we will now learn all of the steps for TRUe breaTH™.

At the beginning of this exercise, everything will be the same as we have already practiced, except towards the end, we will now add in the *magic* of the belly-brain "Godspeed" reflex.

1. *Notice* your state of "being"
2. Close your mouth
3. Eyes open
4. Put your tongue on the roof of your mouth
5. Place your hands on your belly
6. Breathe in through your nose
7. As you breathe in through your nose, stick your belly out
8. Breathe in as much as you can—don't hold back
9. *While holding your breath, let go of your ego, your past, and accept the present moment. Who am I?*
10. The belly is as big as it can get

11. Only your belly moves—make sure not to engage your chest or neck muscles

12. Then as you notice that you need to breath out...*don't*

13. Try to breathe in more without engaging your chest or neck muscles

14. *Only* the belly tries to get bigger

15. *Hold it* in that position until you need to breathe out

16. Then exhale your breath out of your mouth

You now have put it all together. TRUe breaTH™ is not just learning a new technique for breath work. It's a shift, it's *transformational*, it's a new paradigm, it's ***Feel Better*** **Get Well**.

Part 1: Where and When TRUe breaTH™ Should be Performed

The greatest aspect of TRUe breaTH™ is taking back your power to connect with your soul *moment-by-moment*.

When you are going to perform TRUe breaTH™, it should be to *notice* your life *moment-by-moment.*

Notice your feelings, which are your own interpretation from the stressors of life. You are the director, the actor, and the witness to the movie of your life.

What I mean is that you need to start only by just *noticing,* without judgement or without you (or anyone) trying to figure out your "whys," including family, friends and/or medical health practitioners.

If you *notice* that you feel sad, scared, anxious—whatever negative feeling you might have at that moment (remember you're never wrong since it's your life), you're going to perform 1-2 TRUe breaTH™s, without trying to change your feelings.

Just stay in the state of ***being*** and not in the state of ***doing***.

TRUe breaTH™ should be performed every time you *notice* what you have determined to be a negative feeling. Which goes to the next point that TRUe breaTH™ can be performed anywhere; sitting, standing, or lying down and any time during the day.

The simple answer is that to get the best results, perform TRUe breatTH *whenever and wherever* you want to create *transformation* in your life.

Part 2: What's the Prescription—Frequency (Number of Times) and Dosage (Amount of Substance)

The current prescription for mindfulness and meditation requires you to perform it once or twice a day (which is a low frequency) and for 20 minutes at a time (which is a large dosage).

The current model for transformation is a prescription of a low frequency (which means a few times a day) and a high dosage (which means doing each session for a long period of time).

And for all of this, you need to be in a quiet space.

The new prescription for TRUe breaTH™ requires you to perform it numerous times a day—a very high frequency. In fact, the more the better, except it should only be performed for a few minutes at a time, which is a very low dosage.

This prescription is based on homeopathy, which is a centuries-old method of healing based on unseen energetic connections of herbs and plants and hopefully sounds familiar.

The gist of this new homeopathic prescription for TRUe breaTH™ is the opposite frequency and dosage of the current prescription suggested by mindfulness and meditation.

Chapter 7: Summary

Now that you have the knowledge and wisdom of TRUe breaTH™ let's put it all together by parsing out each step and relating it back to the wisdom we have just acquired.

1. Notice your state of being: *Being, doing, having*. We need to start to notice our feelings without judgement.

2. To be present of how we view ourselves moment-by-moment, then start doing *stuff.*

3. Close your mouth: A funny energetic unseen connection is between the mouth and anus, since they look similar. Ever hear of the saying, "talking shit?" So close your mouth—words can't describe your soul.

4. Eyes open: This is unique for breath work; life happens with your eyes open and your feelings can change just by closing them. We want transformation, not change. I've noticed that this can be hard for some people, especially when you do TRUe breaTH™ lying down. Keep them open.

5. Put your tongue on the roof of your mouth. This closes off the oxygen coming from your mouth, and has been shown to cause a downregulation effect on the central nervous system.

6. Place your hands on your belly. This will really help in the beginning to train the physicalness of TRUe breaTH™.

7. Breathe in through your nose; it has a built-in filter, unlike the mouth.

8. As you breathe in through your nose, stick your belly out. This is the embryological connection, the connection to our soul, our purpose, our *truth.*

9. Breathe in as much as you can—don't hold back. This is the automatic unseen connection of the belly and the brain.

10. Let go of your ego, your past and accept the present moment. Who am I? Accept who you are; love, happiness, light etc. Bypassing your mind/brain where past negative thoughts, traumas and shame can be held.

11. The belly is as big as it can get. This is self-explanatory; the bigger the stressors (seen or unseen) the bigger you need to stick out your gut.

12. Only your belly moves—make sure not to engage your chest or neck muscles. If you use the chest and neck you will be using muscles involved with the voluntary musculoskeletal mind/brain system, which will hold you in the past.

13. Hold your belly breath. As you're noticing and then witnessing, what does your mind/brain want you to do to keep you living in the past? The mind/brain is fighting the soul/organ for ownership back and forth.

14. Then as you notice that you need to breathe out, *don't.* There is a moment when your mind/brain is saying carbon dioxide is building up, and now it's time to breathe out so you can breathe in more oxygen. Your mind-brain is fighting for control and is saying, "We have done this before; let's keep living in

the past." We can change over time. Except this time, the soul says, "*Hell no*, we have free will to decide," which causes a resetting of the automatic nervous system using the Belly-Brain Reflex, where the magic of transformation happens moment-by-moment. The soul wins the battle.

15. Try to breathe in more without engaging your chest or neck muscles. I choose, I have free will to command my life moment-by-moment; I will *not* succumb to the mind and, in fact, I'm bypassing the mind. Just to make sure the mind gets the point that the *soul* is in control, we are doing the opposite and attempting to breathe in more.

16. *Only* the belly tries to get bigger, making sure to keep you in the present moment

17. Hold your breath and belly in that position until you need to breathe out. Accept yourself as a King or Queen owning your human spirit—your *truth.*

18. Then exhale your breath out of your mouth. This lets the darkness out—*freedom.*

TRUe breaTH™ = TRUTH

In the name TRUebreaTH™ if you take away the E, B, R, E, and A, it now spells TRUTH.

The E represents your *ego* and dropping your facade and living in the past. The current model, Get Well Feel Better, is to strengthen the ego because someone has the time and patience twice a day to sit still for 20 minutes.

The B represents the *body* and dropping the seen voluntary musculoskeletal structural system as the paradigm to obtain *transformation.*

The R represents reaction and dropping the mind/brain complex to decide your life ***moment-by-moment***.

The E and A represent dropping the *Ego.* Again the mind is so powerful, yet non-existent in the presence of the light of your soul.

My quote is:

"Life Begins with a Breath

Life Ends with a Breath."

WHO, WHAT, WHEN, WHERE and HOW You BREATHe will determine your life.

WHO: *Notice* your state of *being*—Who am I?

WHAT: Automatic nervous system and unseen non-structural energetic connection

WHEN: Embryological model and connection of the belly brain

WHERE: Magic of the Belly-Brain Reflex

HOW: Homeopathic prescription

Notice your feelings from life's stressors, and that's different for everybody. Some people need to *notice* their life 500 times a day because they're so stressed out—no judgement.

The lungs and breathing: Emotions are housed in the organs/belly. The unseen/non-structural energetic automatic nervous system and the connection to the brain.

Utilizing the Belly-Brain Reflex to bypass the mind; the speed of *transformation*/enlightenment *moment-by-moment*.

Do TRUe breaTH™ all throughout the day—at the store, driving, sitting home with the kids, with friends or family, at work to get back to your intuition, to your soul to find your purpose in life whenever and wherever, *moment-by-moment*.

I'm honored and incredibly grateful to share TRUe breaTH. Safe journey to everyone ***moment-by-moment.***

www.ingramcontent.com/pod-product-compliance
Lightning Source LLC
LaVergne TN
LVHW041255150826
845673LV00008B/2601
9798653064388